*Walter S Smith, Jr*

# One-of-a-Kind Judge

## The Honorable
## Hippo Garcia

JOAN COOK CARABIN

**LifeRich**
PUBLISHING
an imprint of The Reader's Digest Association, Inc.

LifeRich Publishing books may be ordered through booksellers or by contacting:

LifeRich Publishing
1663 Liberty Drive
Bloomington, IN 47403
www.liferichpublishing.com
1 (888) 238-8637

Because of the dynamic nature of the Internet, any web addresses or links contained in
this book may have changed since publication and may no longer be valid. The views
expressed in this work are solely those of the author and do not necessarily reflect the views
of the publisher, and the publisher hereby disclaims any responsibility for them.

Any people depicted in stock imagery provided by Thinkstock are models,
and such images are being used for illustrative purposes only.
Certain stock imagery © Thinkstock.

ISBN: 978-1-4897-0139-8 (sc)
ISBN: 978-1-4897-0137-4 (e)

Library of Congress Control Number: 2014902364

Printed in the United States of America.

LifeRich Publishing rev. date: 4/29/2014

# Dedication

*For the children and teens of the public housing courts, family courts, and juvenile justice courts.*

*For every child who needs a voice.*

*For the protective service workers, child advocates, attorneys ad litem and judges standing with and speaking for these children.*

*For every person who needs to find a voice.*

*Hippo Garcia needed a voice and he showed children, teens and adults where and how to find their voices.*

# Contents

# Illustrations

# Foreword

The old adage that goes back to at least the mid-19th century, as seen in the newspaper *Piqua Democrat*, June 1867, and I paraphrase, "Don't judge a book by its cover, see a man by his cloth, as there is often a good deal of solid worth and superior skill beneath the jacket and pants—but in this case, the robe that was his uniform…. The Honorable Hipolito Francisco Garcia, loved and known by all as "Hippo" was a model exemplar of this maxim and he was my "compadre."

Hippo was not a striking or imposing figure physically, nor was he outspoken or aggressive in speech or conversation. His demeanor was muted and retiring and though his presence was not overpowering or demanding, he was highly respected by family, friends, colleagues and the public in general. All who knew him or heard of him as he lived and worked his whole life in the community of San Antonio, came to fully recognize and appreciate him as "the giant" that he was, as a man of high skill, and a great judge of human nature, with all of the pitfalls and weaknesses of all of us as humans, whose lives are affected by births, deaths, illnesses, successes, failures and simply the trials and tribulations of life. He experienced all of those things and lived through the course of his childhood, his upbringing, his military service, his education, his professional life as a lawyer and finally through his dedication to his profession and his community as a judge.

This knowledge and these experiences made a rewarding and indelible impression on him to such a degree that during his lifetime, this impression thus received, was reflected in his dealings with friends and strangers and thousands of accused individuals in minor and horrific offenses that came before him for justice and punishment in connection therewith. He was kind and understanding in his rulings and could be severe also when merited. His thousands of friends, acquaintances and defendants will attest to the "pages" within that misleading "cover" and never forget "Hippo." This "cover" was truly not revealing of the "book" that he was. He will be forever remembered, fondly and humorously recalled and his memory cherished by all those who had the distinct pleasure and honor of calling him "friend."

Ms. Carabin has captured the essence of the man, his life, his work, his profession and his "mark" on our community in her wonderful tribute to H.F. "Hippo" Garcia in this book entitled "One of a Kind Judge Judge."

Roy R. Barrera, Sr.

# *Preface*

Hippo Garcia was born in 1922 and grew up in Lavaca, the oldest living residential neighborhood in San Antonio. He became the first Hispanic appointed Federal Judge of the Western District of Texas. I feel his untold story needs to move beyond family and friends into the coming generations. If today's students and other citizens could imagine an unknown neighbor who by study, work, and friendships helped to create a whole generation of public leaders, could they be encouraged to extend themselves to a wider world? *Honorable Hippo: One of a Kind Judge* shows a way an ordinary person can achieve this.

In 1992 my husband Robert and I moved into 210 Lavaca Street next door to the Garcia family home at 216 Lavaca Street. Here we became friends with the Judge's family members. The Judge came to the family home every Sunday to spend precious time with his terminally ill mother. We were there when my husband celebrated the Last Rites as Hippo's mother was dying. This family encouraged, inspired and delighted us as neighbors and friends. We learned about Judge Garcia through his family rather than through personal contact.

After retiring from teaching English Composition and Literature in the Alamo Colleges, I decided to enroll in the Institute of Children's Literature. When it came time to consider a major project, the story of Judge Garcia and his family was the first topic coming to mind. Henry and Arturo, the Judge's brothers and his sister Olga were all for it. His nephew Judge David Garcia, and his many friends and colleagues cheered the idea and offered to help with it.

When I passed the first United States Federal Courthouse in San Antonio, rededicated in his honor, I asked myself how I could continue to pass on the spirit of helpful friendship which Judge Garcia extended to so many people of all conditions in life and work. So I wrote the book.

JOAN COOK CARABIN

# Acknowledgements

Judge Hippo Garcia's sister, Olga, his brothers Henry and Arturo, and his nephew Judge David J. Garcia made writing this book possible. As the family record keeper, Olga, spent hours sharing what is known of the family history in Mexico and the early years in the USA. She and her son Judge David J. Garcia opened the gateway to most of the other people who contributed their memories and papers of the life and times of the Judge.

Hippos' long time friends and coworkers: Roy R. Barrera Sr., Judge John W. Primomo, Judge Edward C. Prado, Van G. Hilley, Joseph Casseb, Carmen Barrera Ramirez, Margaret Montemayor, Bexar County Criminal District Attorney Susan D. Reed, Maurice West, Steve P. Takas, Oscar Flores, and Hamilton Randell contributed their time and staff to tracking down details of the Judge's life and work.

Manuel Flores, Assistant Principal of Brackenridge High School, and Isabel Dever, Administrator for Policies, Procedures, and Public Information for San Antonio School District, provided records and insights into the young life of H.F. Garcia. ROTC Sponsor Colonel Duane Byrd and ROTC Master Sergeant Rickey Terrell discussed Hippo's hidden capabilities. Al Hartman, Dean of Alumni Affairs St. Mary's Law School, graciously facilitated my first interview in the judicial community with Judge John W. Primomo. Katie Jones, a former Burnet Elementary principal described his visit to "Here Comes the Judge Day" at her school.

Thomas Matt De Waelsche, Texana and Research Department at San Antonio Public Library, went the extra mile to help me use the Micro Fische readers for my print research. To my ever-encouraging friends and editors Pam Slocum and Rebecca Kary, to my instructor Nancy Coffelt from the Institute of Children's Literature where it all started, Stephanie Cornthwaite and Keelyn Walsh at Life Rich Publishing: An imprint of The Reader's Digest Association, Inc. a thousand thanks and one hundred suppers at home will not repay your confidence in me to complete this work of love.

Then there is my light in electronic darkness, Bob, my husband, my faithful computer unscrambler. I married him because he has ever been the best company I could hope to find, a one-of-a-kind sweetheart.

JOAN COOK CARABIN

# Chapter 1

# Three Hipolitos and Where They Came From

THERE WERE THREE HIPOLITO GARCIAS but only one Honorable Judge Hippo Garcia. Judge Hippo's grandfather, Hipolito Garcia #1, was born in 1855 on a ranch near a new town, Villa Acuña, Coahuila, Mexico.

Hipolito Garcia #1's family owned a cattle, sheep and goat ranch. They raised and sold the animals for milk, meat, wool and leather. *Cabrito barbacoa* (young goat or lamb) is a favorite picnic and party cookout in Mexico and South Texas. Their business made a good living for three generations.

In August 1877, Hipolito #1 admired and married Gregoria Rodriguez Garcia, a smart girl from Guerrero Viejo, Coahuila, Mexico. They had three sons together: Jose, Hipolito #2 (b 1890) and Arturo. The boys grew up to be young ranch bosses. Cowboys *(vaqueros)* did all the heavy work outside the house. Housemaids *(criadas)* cooked, served, cleaned, and sewed inside the house and maintained the kitchen garden. From age six or seven, each boy owned a horse and had assigned animals to attend. They enjoyed a comfortable ranch home and good times with friends. Wealthy, healthy, without worries, these boys never imagined how their lives would change in a few years.

Dangerous days and nights started boiling up in Mexico. Working people had to fight for the money they earned. Small farmers and ranchers lost their property to strangers overnight. People wanted a chance to say something about how and where they would live. They wanted education and health care for their children. Modern transportation was almost nonexistent. Starvation and death stalked poor people.

In 1877, the same year Hipolito #1 and Gregoria married, a handsome master problem solver, General Porfirio Diaz won Mexico's presidential election. He made changes rapidly, some for better, others for worse.

Porfirio Diaz bought votes, confiscated property, and jailed his opponents to stay President for thirty years. One night when Hipolito #2 was a teenager, Diaz' soldiers rode out to Hipolito #1's ranch and shouted, "Come outside, goat! Take your old woman and kids. Leave! This place doesn't belong to you anymore. The new owners will come to take charge in the morning."

Hipolito #1 knew that soldiers shot some fathers in their yards in front of wives and children for merely talking to the soldiers about another plan. He knew some priests were tortured, others shot for defending the people, for praying with people, or for teaching people about God. Whole families were forced off their farms into cities so the police could watch them more easily. Hipolito #1 nodded to the soldiers, saying nothing. After leaving harsh warnings, the soldiers galloped away.

Then Hipolito #1 called his family into the front room and said, "My family, tonight we are runaways. We run to save our lives, and to hope for a better future. Sons, pack one bag of clothes each. Mama, take whatever food, supplies, blankets, and kitchen tools you can carry to the wagon outside. Hipolito, Arturo, take our beds and biggest table apart and load them on the largest wagon. Jose, hitch the mules, load firewood, bring up our strongest horses. I will load the hunting rifles and ammunition. I will empty the safe and camouflage whatever is in it. We must camp outside away from here until we can find another place to stay."

Walking away under the starlight, they left behind their home, memories, and everything they had built up together. They praised and thanked God because all of them were alive. They had each other.

Many family things, including the only photograph of Hipolito #1, and a thank you letter from Judge Roy Bean were lost, stolen or burned during these years. One handwritten financial ledger showing they had thirty-seven employees on the ranch survived. The descendants do not know where this family lived or how long they camped outdoors. The descendants have been unable to pinpoint the exact location of the family ranch because property records were burned during the Revolution.

Meanwhile, everything families needed: food, milk, clothes, shoes, tools, seeds, medicine, books, became scarcer and more expensive. Hipolito #1 died suddenly. Gregoria, now alone, stood strong with three young boys.

Gregoria read the newspapers daily. She listened to her neighbors' reports. She saw the dangers growing worse. Soon the Mexican government would make war on its own citizens. The Mexican Revolution began in the South and slowly moved to the North. Many honest people would die. The fires of war would ruin ranches, schools, businesses, churches, and towns.

Teenage boys without fathers or bribe money would be forced to fight and to die. Tween boys would be kidnapped to train for war. Some girls hid in cellars whenever they heard soldiers' horses approaching. Other teenage girls would be raped, tortured, killed. Some girls armed themselves to fight with their brothers. Gregoria saw it; she heard it; she felt it creeping closer. She stood against it and planned their escape.

After writing a short letter to her sister-in-law, Virginia Garcia in Piedras Negras, she sent Hipolito #2 and Jose to visit their Aunt Virginia's home, a short walk over the dusty footbridge from Eagle Pass, Texas.

Later, a trusted friend reported to her that the secret police wanted Arturo for something he had written in opposition to the government. Gregoria packed a camelback trunk with a blanket, clothing and food, and loaded it on a wagon. Gregoria and Arturo headed to Piedras. An unknown sniper shot her in the stomach on the road. Details of her recovery are unknown, but her strong spirit survived 79 years until October, 1942.

Gregoria Rodriguez Garcia and her sons understood their Piedras Negras visit was temporary. She said, "I intend for my sons to have an education and a normal future in Texas." One by one, the four of them left quietly for San Antonio. Gregoria became a permanent U.S. resident in 1915. In 1917 she rented a house at 126 Wyoming Street, a short walk from downtown San Antonio.

For a while she sent the boys as boarders to St. Louis School about six miles out in the country to learn English. Hipolito #2 learned quickly. Soon he spoke some English. He didn't like living away from home. Because he wanted to work and to help his mother financially, he ran away from school more than once.

The boys found work quickly: Jose as a store clerk, Hipolito #2 as a butcher for the Menger Hotel, and Arturo as a baker for the Menger Hotel. They worked hard. Arturo attended night school to become a certified baker. Later Hipolito #2 was promoted to chef at the Menger and the St. Anthony Hotel, both upscale, historic hotels.

Some relatives felt bad to see one time rich teenage boys working in stores and hotel kitchens. But these boys felt proud to help their mother. Together they saved enough money and March 3, 1923, Gregoria bought a limestone home at 216 Lavaca Street, now part of the National Historic Trust. For 89 years different members of the Garcia family have lived there. Today Henry Garcia, younger brother of Hipolito #3, lives and works there.

Hipolito Garcia #2 met Francisca Sanchez. Her father could not afford to support his daughter at home in Mexico, but he knew a kind woman on Martinez St. in San Antonio who wanted help in the house. At age thirteen Francisca went to live with the new family. She worked as a *criada* (housemaid). She never again saw anyone from her own family, but the homeowner loved her like a daughter. Although this helped ease her homesickness, it caused friction with the American daughters.

Eventually Hipolito and Francisca married. December 4, 1925, at age 35, Hipolito #2 and Francisca became the parents of Hipolito Garcia #3. June 7, 1926 he was baptized at San Fernando Cathedral, San Antonio's spiritual home base.

## New People:

Porfirio Diaz born in Oaxaca, Mexico, 1830–1915. Elected President of Mexico 1877, served one three year term as he promised. Reelected 1884, reneged on promise and continued in office by illegal means until 1911.

Judge Roy Bean never attended law school. He named himself "the only law west of the Pecos." Relying on a copy of the 1879 Revised Statues of Texas, he held court in his Jersey Lilly Saloon, Langtry, Texas for twenty years.

## New Places and Things:

Ciudad Acuña, also known as Las Vacas or Villa Acuña, is a city in northern Coahuila *estado* (state), northeastern Mexico. This city is on the Rio Grande also known as *Rio Bravo del Norte* across the U.S. Mexico border from Del Rio, Texas. Ciudad Acuña is a port of entry and a commercial and manufacturing center for the agricultural area surrounding it. Wheat, nuts, sheep and goats are raised. A railroad and highway connect Acuña with other locations in Coahuila and Texas. The area population is about 126,238.

*Cabrito,* a kid goat up to one year old. A tender, savory meal served barbecued.

Guerrero Viejo. The inhabitants of Guerrero Viejo moved to a new town, Ciudad Guerrero in the 1950s due to flooding of their town and of Zapata, Texas caused by building Amistad Dam and the rising waters of the newly created Falcon Lake.

Piedras Negras is called *La Puerto de Mexico* (Mexico's Door) because of the constant flow of commercial traffic and people that cross both sides of the Rio Grande River through it. Piedras Negras' sister city is Eagle Pass, Texas. Both are known for their ranches where avid sport lovers hunt exotic game.

St. Louis School was a Catholic boarding school for teenage boys in San Antonio. This school developed into the present-day St. Mary's University and Law School.

# Chapter 1: Works Consulted

"Ciudad Acuña." Encyclopedia Britannica Online. 2011. Encyclopedia Britannica. <http://www.britannica.com/ /topic/119121/Ciudad-Acuna>

"Ciudad Acuña." <http://en.wikipedia.org/wiki/Ciudad_Acu%C3%B1a>

Ciudad Acuña's municipal website <http://www.acuna.gob.mx>

Ciudad Acuña's social website <http://www.acuna.gob.mx>

Garcia, Arturo. Telephone interview. 16 May 2011.

"Judge Roy Bean and others on porch of Jersey Lilly, Langtry, TX." Photograph ca. 1900, #71 UTSA.

"Judge Roy Bean's Jersey Lilly Saloon in Langtry, Texas." Photograph. <http://www.legendsofamerica.com/picturepages/PP-OldWest1.html>

Minister, Christopher. "The Mexican Revolution: Ten Years That Forged a Nation." Latin American History. <www.about.com>

Minister, Christopher. "How Did Porfirio Diaz Stay in Power for 35 Years?" Latin American History. <www.about.com>

Moore, Lucy. Anything Goes: A Biography of the Roaring Twenties. New York: Overland Press, 2010.

Overfelt, Robert C. "Mexican Revolution." "Mexican Texans in the Civil War." The New Handbook of Texas. Texas State Historical Association, 1996. 686–689.

"Piedras Negras." <http://luaposada.tourbymexico.com/coahuila/pidrnegr/piedrasn.htm>

Rodriguez, Olga Garcia. Personal interview. 5 Jan. 2011.

Rodriguez, Olga Garcia. Personal interview. 31 Jan. 2011.

Rodriguez, Olga Garcia. Personal interview. 12 May 2011.

Rodriguez, Olga Garcia. Personal interview. 5 Oct. 2011.

Rodriguez, Olga Garcia. Handwritten notes. 27–31 January 2011.

San Antonio City Directory. 1923–1925.

Unsigned, "PorfirioDiaz—from Military Hero to Dictator," MEXonline.com. <www.riograndeguardian.com>

# Chapter 2

# School Days at Burnet, Poe and Brackenridge

ALTHOUGH THEIR FATHER, HIPOLITO #2, learned English at St. Louis School, all the Garcias spoke Spanish at home. Grandmother Gregoria and mother Francisca couldn't go to school to study English. In those days there were few English classes for grownups anywhere in Texas.

That was bad news. For over 100 years educators believed bilingual education was educational medicine for poor and disadvantaged students, not a tool for developing the language abilities of all the students. Worse, federal courts built rulings on the idea that students who spoke other languages had a handicap to be overcome. Children were punished for speaking Spanish in school or on the playground. Toward the end of the twentieth century, lawmakers and educators began to realize that students speaking two or more languages had more ideas, more vocabulary, more friends and more opportunities.

Hippo #3 said, "When I started first grade, it was sink or swim. I thought the English word for bathroom was 'cuseplease.' All the other kids raised their hands saying, 'cuseplease.' So I did too. They meant, 'Excuse me, please.'" Only three blocks from home, school felt like a strange land.

"On my worst day, we got out at noon, and I had to wait outside for mother until 3:00 PM because I didn't understand teacher's announcement the day before. Few of our teachers ever spoke Spanish."

Looking at Hippo's Burnet Elementary Permanent Record Card (see p. 11) from ages 5–10 (1932–1937) we can see how hard he studied from year to year.

Hippo's record at Edgar Allan Poe Junior School (see p. 12) shows a young man arriving every day on time, working steadily for the progress he makes. There's no magic brain here. He's no sports superstar either.

Olga Garcia Rodriguez is Hippo's only sister. She said, "I was the lone girl with five brothers: Hipolito, Roberto, Raul, and Enrique, all were older. Arturo was six years younger than me. Our family called Hipolito, 'Polo.' A junior high school friend started calling him Hippo, and it stuck for life."

Arturo Garcia, Hippo's youngest brother, remembers at first Hippo didn't like his nickname. He changed his mind saying, "With so many Garcias here, a name like Hippo will stand out." Now that name shines. One time a new secretary asked another secretary, "What's Hippo's last name?" He turned around laughing and said, "Potamus."

Hippo's brother Henry remembers, "I was five years old when Hippo took me to my first movie." Henry, 80, is the fourth brother, a shy type, but he flashes a young smile when he remembers the day Hippo called, "Hurry up or we'll be late for Gene Autry." Henry said, "We wanted to see Gene's show at the Plaza Theatre. I let him lead the way up Alamo Street because I knew he knew more about the town.

"When we got there, my mouth opened like a baby bird's. I saw this giant neon sign of a cowboy twirling his lasso, chasing a little dogie, missing him every time, then starting again. That bubbling sign was a show before the show.

"Then he took me to see all the cowboy posters outside before we went inside the beautiful lobby to pay our 10¢ admission and 5¢ popcorn. We saw many more flashy posters inside the lobby.

## Judge 'Hippo'

Judge Hippo Garcia, as he is universally known, examines models of his favorite animal. Numerous pictures and likenesses adorn his office, all gifts from friends. The nickname "Hippo" was acquired in elementary school. The story of how it happened is on Pg. 4-A.

# Hippos of all shapes keep judge company

...when Anglo chil-

*Judge Garcia Displays His Collection*

"When we sat down inside the theatre, I was speechless. There were more chairs than in church, more seats than in gym, or benches at baseball. The ceiling was high as a circus tent and painted all over. This was the biggest room I ever sat in, and suddenly it turned pitch dark. Yes, darker than nighttime, darker than our next door neighbor Oscar Yznaga's cellar, darker than the tunnel to the Alamo my dad showed me. I lost my breath, then I began crying, yelling, 'Daddy, help!' and I couldn't stop. Hippo tried to quiet me, but I wouldn't listen to him."

His sister Olga said, "The main thing I remember about Hippo was he loved reading more than all our uncles, brothers, and cousins did. After dark, he'd go under the covers with a flashlight to read. Sometimes he'd lock himself in a bedroom to study. When it came time for high school, Hippo chose Brackenridge even though all our other brothers went to Fox Tech. Hippo insisted on Brack. He was one of a handful of Hispanics in the ROTC (Reserved Officers Training Corps) and treasurer of the Pan American Club."

Current Brackenridge High School administrators admit their predecessors did not recognize Hippo's potential. He did not qualify for the National Honor Society or Sigma Epsilon Society. Even so, he was one of nine out of 500 Brackenridge graduates on May 28, 1943, with perfect attendance. Studying Hippo's final Brackenridge Cumulative Record (see p. 13), you might wonder, what kind of person ignores every excuse for missing school? This average kid completed four years work in six semesters. Was he driven to do it?

# Burnet Elementary—Permanent Record

| Year and Age | Final Grade | | Days Attended | |
|---|---|---|---|---|
| | 1st. term | 2nd. term | 1st. term | 2nd.term |
| 1931–32  5 | — | B | — | 68 |
| 1932–33  6 | C | B | 80 | 82 |
| 1933–34  7 | C | B | 88 | 83.5 |
| 1934–35  8 | B | B | 80 | 87 |
| 1935–36  9 | B | B | 80 | 86 |
| 1936–37  10 | A | A | 86 | 90 |
| Remarks: Promoted to Poe Middle School | | | | |

# *Poe Junior High—Permanent Record*

| SUBJECTS | 6B | 6A | SUBJECTS | 7B | 7A | SUBJECTS | 8B | 8A |
|---|---|---|---|---|---|---|---|---|
| English | B | B+ | English | A– | A | English | B– | B |
| Literature | | A | Literature | A | B+ | Literature | D | C |
| Health Education | D | F | Health Education | F | B | Health Education | F | C+ |
| Social Studies | B | B | Social Studies | B | A | Social Studies | A | C+ |
| Mathematics | D | B– | Mathematics | C | D | Mathematics | | |
| Nature Study | | B | | | | | | |
| | | | | | | General Science | B | |
| Speech Arts | | | | A– | C | | | |
| | | | Spanish | | B | Spanish | B+ | A |
| Music | | B+ | Music | A– | | Music | A– | A |
| Mech. Drawing | C | | | | | | | |
| Wood Work | | C+ | | | | | | |
| | | | | | | Library Science | | A |
| | | | | | | Home Room | A | |
| Days Present | 90 | 85 | Days Present | 77 | 85 | Days Present | 85 | 91 |
| Days Absent | 0 | 0 | Days Absent | 0 | 0 | Days Absent | 0 | 0 |
| Times Tardy | 0 | 0 | Times Tardy | 0 | 0 | Times Tardy | 0 | 0 |

6A Book monitor (Social Studies), Assembly (2)

7B Assembly, Treasurer of Home Room

7A

8B Lead in Assembly, Captain of C.C.

# Brackenridge High School—Record Card

| Year | Fall 1940 | Spring 1941 | Fall 1941 | Spring 1942 | Fall 1942 | Spring 1943 |
|---|---|---|---|---|---|---|
|  |  |  |  |  |  |  |
|  |  |  |  |  |  |  |
| English | III B | IV A | V B | VI B | VII B | VIII B |
| English |  |  |  |  |  | IX B |
| Algebra | I C | II D | III D | IV D |  |  |
| World History | I A | II B |  |  |  |  |
| American History |  |  |  |  | I B | II A |
| Civics |  |  | I A |  |  |  |
| Texas History |  |  |  |  |  | C |
| Spanish | III C | IV A | V A | VI C |  |  |
| Chemistry |  |  |  |  | I C | II D |
| Journalism |  |  |  | I B | II B |  |
| R.O.T.C. | B | B | B | A | C |  |
|  |  |  |  |  |  |  |
| TOTAL CREDITS | 13 | 18 | 23 | 28 | 33 | 38 |
|  |  |  |  |  |  |  |
|  | 9/10/43— Sent transcript to St. Mary's University Downtown College, 112 College Street. |  |  |  |  |  |
|  |  |  |  |  |  |  |
|  | 2/4/44—Sent transcript to him at 216 Lavaca Street for Army purposes. |  |  |  |  |  |

## New People:

Gene Autry, 1907-1998. America's first singing cowboy on radio, records, film, television and live theatre including rodeo.

## New Places:

Burnet Elementary School, 406 Barrera Street, is three blocks from 216 Lavaca Street.

Poe Middle School, 814 Aransas Avenue, is two miles from 216 Lavaca. Begun in 1923 E.A. Poe was the first junior high school west of the Mississippi River.

Brackenridge High School, one of two San Antonio public high schools in the 1920s–30s, is college preparatory having many advanced placement classes.

Fox Tech High School, one of two San Antonio public high schools in the 1920s–30s, is vocational and technical having many preprofessional programs.

Plaza Theatre, located at the corner of Alamo and Blum, from 1894 to 1939, was sold to Joske's Department Store. The neon sign on the roof of the Plaza Theatre is believed to have been the largest in Texas during 1930s.

The Garcia and Yznaga brothers staged boxing matches in Oscar Yznaga's cellar.

# Chapter 2: Works Consulted

Allen, Paula. " Sold to Joske's." *San Antonio Express-News*. Images. 27 Aug. 1995. p. 15.

Cude, Elton. "Plaza Theatre." *San Antonio Light* Oct. 1978. San Antonio Conservation Society, file Theatres H–P.

Dever, Isabel. Administrator for Policies, Procedures, and Public Information, San Antonio Independent School District. Personal interview. 6 May 2011.

Garcia, Arturo. Telephone interview. 16 May 2011.

Garcia, Henry. Personal interview. 14 April 2011.

Garcia, Henry. Personal interview. 12 May 2011.

Garcia, Henry. Telephone interview. 24 April 2011.

Gene Autry official website, 1907–1998. <http://www.autry.com/> <http:/www.cowboypal.com/>

"Plaza Theatre." Photographs. Institute of Texan Cultures, UTSA, L0294-A, L0955-A, L201-A, CD 180, L 1559-RR, 93-524, courtesy of the Hearst Corp.

"Robert Garcia in costume." Photograph. *Forever Texas: Historical Photographs and More.* #44L3656 C. <http://digital.utsa.edu/cdm4/browse.php?CISOROOT=%2Fp9020coll008>

"Judge Roy Bean and others on porch of Jersey Lilly." Photograph. Langtry, TX ca. 1900. #71

Poe Middle School. <http://www.saisd.net/schools/poe054/index.php?option=com_content&view=section&id=8&Itemid=30>

Rivera, Tomas. *Y no se lo trago la tierra: And the Earth Did Not Devour Him.* Houston: Arte Publico Press, 1992.

Rodriguez, Olga Garcia. Personal interview. 6 January 2011.

Rodriguez, Olga Garcia. Personal interview. 31 January 2011.

Rodriguez, Olga Garcia. Personal interview. 12 May 2011.

"Texas Escapes." Online Magazine. <http://TexasEScapes.com>

Texas Historic Theaters. <http://www.lhat.org/historictheatres/theatre_inventory/Texas.aspx>

# Chapter 3

# The World Opens Up

HIPPO ENLISTED IN THE UNITED States Army one day before his eighteenth birthday, 1943. Homesick, scared, excited. Basic Training at Ft. Chaffee, Arkansas was unlike Brackenridge High School. During the first inspection lineup, the Drill Sergeant saw how shy Hippo looked and shouted, "What's your name Soldier?" Going blank Hippo couldn't remember. He looked up, saw a name plate on the Sergeant's uniform, and yelled back "Frank." Later he revised that story saying, "I took Frank as my middle name for my mother, Francisca." In court he signed his cases H. F. Garcia.

The friendly learning atmosphere of Brackenridge High School changed to formal training for war. Getting up before sunrise, long and hard physical training, wearing drab uniforms for physical exercise, wearing different uniforms for work details, sports, and dress occasions, lining up and saluting were a few of the outward, visible changes Hippo made.

The inner, invisible changes in mind, heart and spirit came like shaking up a snow globe, waiting to see where the pieces would fall. In boot camp, using his analytical, creative mind was not a high priority. Instead, following directions, responding quickly without arguing, exerting and expanding his physical strength counted the most. Hippo Garcia never performed well in sports, so this part cost him. Protecting other soldiers from danger became as important as guarding his own safety. He learned teamwork and the buddy system, both new to him.

In training he used live ammunition, practiced in fields, deserts and mountains, slept outside on the ground in rain, snow and heat. There were no air-conditioned tents and no indoor toilets or showers. Most foods were rehydrated from dry packets like the free breakfast motel oatmeal. He could not be choosy because soldiers have no other choices.

After boot camp Hippo transferred to the Third Armored Spearhead Division fighting in France and Germany. There he became a M4 Sherman tank driver. Before enlisting, using the family car in town equaled his total driving experience. The first day on the new job he had to ask someone to show him where to fill the gas tank.

His Third Armored Division had trained in every kind of climate, but nowhere had they seen terrain like the hedgerows. Wild, thick, mound-like rows of scrub undergrowth grew 8 to 10 feet in width and 4 to 6 feet in height. The length varied from place to place. Thick trees grew along the tops of these rows. A ditch ran along one or both sides of the rows. Narrow, winding roads ran between the hedgerows giving the enemy many positions to ambush advancing soldiers.

Hippo's job was driving an armored Sherman tank over and around the hedgerows. He was responsible for his own safety and for the other soldiers inside: the assistant driver/ bow gunner, the gunner, the ammunition loader/gunner, assistant gunner, and the Tank Commander/gunner. Everyone communicated by hand signals.

Normally, because of the hedgerows height, his vision was limited from one hedgerow to the next. A fixed periscope helped a little. His instrument panel contained gauges for speed, oil pressure, and fuel, plus a starter switch, a circuit breaker, a tachometer and two utility outlets. Most of these were entirely new to him. This 18-year-old, inexperienced driver was controlling a 19-foot-long, 8-foot-wide, and 9-foot-high war machine weighing 31.3 tons, armed with three machine guns, and one long gun. Up-gunned Sherman tanks also packed smoke mortars and flame throwers.

Being in the Spearhead Division gave Hippo many opportunities to be first in military action. Some of their accomplishments included:

»   First to cross the Belgian border 2 September 1944

»   First to fire an artillery shell into Germany 11 September 1944

»   First Division to cross the German border, east of Eupen 11 September 1944

»   First to capture a German town in this war, Roetgen 12 September 1944

»   First to breach the Siegfried Line 13 September 1944

»   First American division to completely pierce the Siegfried Line 15 September 1944

»   First to shoot down an enemy plane from German soil 18 September 1944

»   First to capture a major German City (Cologne) 5 March 1945

»   First to accomplish the greatest one day advance in mobile warfare (101 miles) 29 March 1945

»   First invasion of Germany in force since Napoleon

Their Commander, Major General Maurice Rose wrote of these men, "The achievements of this Division have been equaled by only a few, and surpassed by none. Our standards are high and our determination to meet those standards is firm. With Divine assistance, little can delay, and nothing can stop us."

Experiencing so many daring and dangerous firsts at ages 18–21 changed Hippo for life. He fought with the bravest men. Together, they outsmarted the cruelest enemies. Fear lost power over him. He let go of his fear, and he released his teenage shyness. From this time forward he chose smart, brave thinkers for friends. By enlarging his goals he would be able try out new ideas after the war ended.

Hippo Garcia emerged alive from the dreadful Battle of the Bulge although his Commander, Major General Maurice Rose, died in the fight. Rose was the only American armored division commander killed in battle during World War II. He was the son and grandson of rabbis and he rose from private to general. He led the premier American armored force to victory over the Nazi empire. Hippo decided that his commander's death would not be pointless. He decided he'd live to serve people. How to do this remained his unanswered question for now.

World War II ended officially 2 September 1945. Decades of cleanup and reconstruction, healing and recovery followed. Hippo received his discharge 19 May 1946. September the same year he registered at St. Mary's University using the GI Bill to help pay for his tuition, fees, and books. Only the freshman report card survived showing a 3.33 average. Little has been written about Hippo's days at St. Mary's. People remember him as a quiet student who made the most of his study time. Again, this student's potential was invisible to his instructors.

Hippo worked part time selling shoes and cleaning a car dealership to pay bills. His St. Mary's classmate, Attorney Roy Barrera, Sr., remembers, "Hippo's goal was to become a manager of a shoe store or a car dealership. He never promoted himself; he concealed how smart he really was." After two years at St. Mary's University, Roy decided to transfer to St. Mary's Law School, and Hippo decided to do the same thing.

Eric Terry wrote this story:

> To help pay his way through law school, Judge Garcia worked as a janitor at St. Mary's. One day during his third year, he was sweeping the floor in the law library when a first year student approached him, looked around, and commented,
>
> "There sure are lots of books."
>
> Hippo Garcia agreed.
>
> Then the student looked at him and asked,
>
> "Did you finish high school?"
>
> Garcia replied that he had.
>
> The student countered,

"Well, that's good because a lot of you people don't graduate."

Later in the week Hippo was asked to give a speech to the first year class. While talking, he observed the student from the library sitting in the front row. The student's expression demonstrated that he finally believed that Hippo Garcia (one of "those people") had finished high school. High School, university and law school were just the beginning for him. He always said, "Education helps a lot, but you need to keep working on a goal."

His University is famous for receiving many awards for volunteers, service learning, and civic commitment. St. Mary's was one of six schools in the United States to be on the 2010 President's Higher Education Community Service Honor Roll. St. Mary's environment, like his brave family, and the United States Army, influenced Hippo for life. The friends he made at St. Mary's helped to raise up a man who improved his city and state, a man who gave help and courage to many students and young professionals.

Graduation from law school does not entitle the graduate to practice law. Passing a long, hard professional examination written by working lawyers and professors is required. After graduation from St. Mary's School of Law, Hippo took the State Bar Examination and was admitted to the Texas State Bar Association. However, no law firm invited him to join. No one guessed his hidden ability. After applying for a job with the District Clerk, the person who files and protects all the county records, he started working there.

## New People

The Spearhead Division was the 3rd Armored Division, a heavy mechanized division of the United States Army, that served in World War Two, the Cold War defense of Western Europe, and the Persian Gulf War. The 3rd Armored Division was reduced to zero strength in 1992, but not inactivated.

Major General Maurice Rose (November 26, 1899—March 30, 1945) is called World War II's Greatest Forgotten Commander. A fictionalized version of his wartime journal came out in 2004. It provides an account of his command of the Third Armored Division during the climactic western European campaign of World War II, the hedgerow fighting in Normandy and more.

## New Places

Belgium borders the North Sea, between France and the Netherlands. It was occupied by the German Army in World War II.

Eupen is a Belgian municipality in the Belgium province of Liege, about nine miles from the German border. After World War II, the Treaty of Versailles transferred Eupen and its neighbor Malmedy from Germany back to Belgium.

Roetgen was the first German town to fall to the allies in World War II.

Siegfried Line was a system of German pillboxes and strong points built along the German western frontier in the 1930s and greatly expanded in 1944. German troops retreating from France used it as a barrier for relief against the pursuing Americans. This helped the Germans mount their counter offensive in the Ardennes Forest. The Allies could not break through the entire line until early 1945.

Cologne, Germany is the fourth largest city in Germany and largest city of the state of North Rhine-Westphalia. One of the key inland ports of Europe, it is the historic, cultural, and economic capital of the Rhineland.

# Chapter 3: Works Consulted

"Cologne." *Encyclopædia Britannica*. 2012 <http://www.britannica.com/EBchecked/topic/125964/Cologne>

Ossad, Stephen L., and Donald. L. Marsh. "Major General Maurice Rose: World War II's Greatest Forgotten Commander." <http://www.stevenlossad.com>

"Siegfried Line." *Encyclopedia Britannica*. 2012 <http://www.britannica.com/EBchecked/topic/543250/Siegfried-Line>

Staff writer. "MF Sherman (Medium Tank, M4)." 18 November 2010 <http://MF Military Factory.com>

Staff writer. "Call Me Spearhead: Saga of the Third Armored Spearhead Division." *Stars and Stripes Publications*, Information and Education Division, Special and Information Services, ETOUSA, 1944. Print.

Staff writer. "Fighting in Normandy." *Combat Lessons,* No. 4. 2007 <www.lonesentry.com>

Terry, Eric. "Just a Closer Walk with Thee Honorable Hippo." *San Antonio Lawyer.* September/October 2000: 6–13. Print.

# Chapter 4

# Hippo's Calling

BEING A LAWYER MEANS WORKING to solve one side of a legal problem. Another lawyer represents the other side. The legal questions are like opposite sides of a tug of war. It is as complicated as a game of chess. Legal problems fall into two large categories: civil cases and criminal cases.

In a civil case, two or more people disagree on important facts in their relationship. Usually money or property is involved. Attorneys on each side present their clients' facts based on the testimony and evidence allowed into court by the judge. A jury decides whose facts are the believable ones, and their decision is called the verdict.

A criminal case results when a person is accused of committing a crime. The accused person is presumed innocent. The State government, represented by the District Attorney, must prove guilt "beyond a reasonable doubt." Jurors decide whether the person charged is guilty or innocent.

Hippo's St. Mary's Law School classmate attorney, Roy Barrera, Sr., tried to persuade Hippo to resign his secure job with Hart McCormick, the District Clerk, and to apply for an assistant's job at the District Attorney's office.

The District Clerk's office was Hippo's safe place, but it stopped him from moving into criminal law where he would become a personal legend. His safe place blocked him from moving out into another life. God's "calling" for him was how Hippo expressed it. He was stuck where he was like a car in mud with the engine running. He started asking himself, "Could this place be too safe? As long as I stay at the district clerk's office I can never be a practicing attorney." Clerking is a good job, but not a lawyer's work.

Roy told him more than once, "You are an attorney!"

Hippo answered, "But I like what I'm doing."

A shy young man, never a self promoter, he told Roy that an assistant district attorney's job was beyond his ability.

"I could never do what they do," he said.

Roy insisted, "You are more than capable."

Finally, Hippo took Roy seriously, applied for the job and was hired. He received five promotions in eight years and became First Assistant District Attorney, and Chief Prosecutor. This promotion surprised some people considering the twenty-six other experienced assistant district attorneys already working there. According to his attorney friend Van Hilley, Hippo was not a gifted speaker. Nevertheless, Van Hilley believes Hippo was the original "Little Boy Who Could." When Hilley was asked, "Who really launched Hippo?" he answered, "No one would ever take credit for that. Hippo did it himself. His family did not do it; his friends did not do it. He kept at it from the time he was a small child who could not speak English. He became proficient in English at Brackenridge High School."

Hippo's boss, District Attorney Charles Lieck, survived a horrible car accident; his voice box was crushed. Never again could he speak in a normal way. As First Assistant District Attorney, Hippo had to speak for the DA, taking his place in legal meetings and press briefings.

Judge Archie Brown often disagreed with District Attorney Lieck's methods. Brown opened an investigation of Lieck's employee, Investigator Albert Weschler. Weschler was accused of selling confidential information to defense attorneys. No investigation was opened against the attorneys buying the information. These are felony crimes. Roy Barrera thought that was unfair and decided to defend Weschler.

Hippo found himself in a mess of confusion and conflicts. He called his position "the hot spot." Working in the same office were: Hippo Garcia First Assistant District Attorney, Investigator Albert Weschler (the man on trial), Roy Barrera (Weschler's defense attorney), Texas Assistant Attorney General Frank Maloney (Weschler's prosecutor), and Bexar County District Attorney Charles Lieck (the boss of Garcia, Barrera and Weschler), soon to be investigated himself. What a steep challenge to Hippo's ability to be fair with everyone involved. Weschler was found guilty. Because nothing was done to investigate the attorneys buying the information, Barrera reopened the case and reversed the judgment against Weschler.

Soon authorities accused Lieck himself of not sending cases to court on time.

Hippo was summoned before the Grand Jury and questioned about late and missing cases.

"Mr. Garcia, do you know where cases W, X, Y, and Z are?"

"Yes, Sir, they are in my desk file drawer." Hippo answered.

"What are they doing in your desk?"

"Mr. Lieck asked me to hold those cases for him, Sir."

"What are these cases about?"

"I don't know, Sir. I have not read them."

"What do you mean, you have not read them? You are First Assistant DA!"

"Sir, Mr. Lieck asked me to hold the cases for him, and I did. That's all I know about the cases."

This might sound innocent, but it could be criminal. If it was found to be Obstruction of Justice, it could end Hippo Garcia's new law career. Obstruction of Justice means hampering the court's work by holding files, hiding files, threatening or bribing witnesses. All these actions are felony crimes. The Grand Jury believed Hippo. They respected the way this young lawyer managed the office business and fifty-five professionals working there. They saw him remain loyal to his supervisor throughout Mr. Lieck's personal and legal problems. When asked about this ordeal Hippo replied, "I went before the Grand Jury sixteen times," he said quietly, "but everything worked out all right."

First Assistant District Attorney Garcia found another friend during his years in the district attorney's office, Judge John F. Onion, Jr. While Judge Onion was district judge for a murder case being tried in his court, Roy Barrera, Sr., was the defense attorney and Hippo Garcia was the prosecutor. Barrera spoke in elaborate detail about his "innocent defendant." He pictured all the mighty law enforcers of Texas swooping down upon this innocent man.

Hippo Garcia, the prosecutor, stood up and looked at the burned-out jurors. "Please relax. I will not take an hour to talk to you like Mr. Barrera did. In fifteen minutes, I will run out of English."

The jurors started laughing.

"Mr. Barrera has spent a great deal of time talking about the power and might of the State of Texas. I represent the State of Texas. I am an overweight Mexican with a crazy-looking tie. Do I really look like the power and might of Texas?" This time the jurors roared with laughter. They convicted the murderer.

Phil Chavarria and Crawford Reeder invited Hippo to join their law firm after he completed 11 years and 6 months at the District Attorney's office. He accepted their offer and clients flocked to him. Before a year was up, he had a successful practice. This private firm became a new safe place. By the end of the first year, he realized he was being called back into government work. This was the only place where he felt he could serve all the people.

During his years (1952–1964) in the Bexar County District Attorney's office, Hippo Garcia got the reputation of a tough prosecutor. He wanted justice for all victims of crime. Voters recognized this attitude and elected him Judge, Bexar County Court-at-Law # 2 in 1964. They appreciated the Judge's capacity to care about all the people. James McCrory reported the election. Garcia carried independent liberals, moderates, labor and conservatives. Numerous PTA's, father and mother groups knew him. Hippo would say he stood with Democrats, Republicans and Vegetarians.

He accepted guilty pleas from five defendants his first day as Judge. He handed down two sentences for child desertion 10–60 days, theft of a radio 10 days, unlawfully carrying a pistol 30 days.

U.S. District Judge James R. Nowlin of Austin, the Western District's Chief Judge, a friend of Hippo's for thirty-five years remembered: "We were both young lawyers and he was at County Court-at-Law #2. We'd go to the gym, and then we'd go out and eat supper. We'd do that every day. Hippo was not ambitious for himself. He was a fantastic judge of people, his street smarts were worthy of an honorary degree."

Maurice West, his court reporter and driver at Bexar County Court-at-Law #2, asked Judge Garcia: "Why do you spend time with young people when you have so many older, more experienced friends?" Judge Garcia said, "The older ones talk about their wives and kids. The younger ones have different ideas about the law, about life." He absorbed the language of youth. Exploring ideas with them helped them to clarify their thoughts, and make their ideas workable in a practical way.

Maurice West believed that Judge Garcia "learned all his life. He hunted learning like a lifetime adventure. At the same time he held back how much he knew, concerned about embarrassing others. The man had a nonstop sense of humor making it easier to be ones true self and making learning easier for everyone around him."

According to West many law students asked the Judge for money to get them "over a financial hump." Although the money was graciously lent, West never saw or heard of one person returning any of the money. Whenever people joined him for lunch or dinner, Hippo always paid. He was generous with everything he had. As a result, Judge Garcia "was more broke than flush, worked from payday to payday, never bought a home of his own, always lived simply in apartments."

People in trouble and people facing road blocks came to see the Judge to ask for his advice or influence. Maurice West said Hippo never, ever broke laws but explained legal ways through and around the obstacles holding people back. What a surprise when he'd recite long passages of Shakespeare or play the piano. Studying Shakespeare gave him a deeper understanding of the dark side of human nature. Playing the piano made him quicker and lighter mentally.

Judge John Primomo, an attorney at the time, considers Judge Hippo a second father and mentor, and says, "Hippo showed great respect for everyone in court: criminals, victims, judges, and attorneys. At the same time, it was easy for him to punish those who had harmed others. He was gifted in recognizing right from wrong." Hippo gained insight into people by listening carefully. He carefully studied all information available on the history, parents, spouse, children, work and social life of the accused. He read every report on every case. He took all details into account in sentencing.

Judge Primomo continues, "After sentencing, he often asked criminals about their families." He understood how the spouses and children of criminals suffer for crimes they never committed. He was a judge who would give a shorter sentence to a criminal he knew would turn his life around. They would pass the word to each other about having a "good chance" if you got Judge Garcia in court.

One day on the way to lunch, Judge Primomo asked Hippo why he always gave money to street people. Without blinking Hippo turned saying, "That could be Jesus." He wasn't taking any chances. Every Christmas season, Judge Primomo walks around San Antonio looking for homeless people. He gives them gifts saying, "This is for you from Judge Garcia."

Attorney Clem Lyons gives Hippo credit for teaching him "the art of jury selection, the art of cross-examination, and the art of the closing argument." Mr. Lyons gives Hippo the credit for leading the way to democratize the judiciary in South Texas.

Bill Blagg says, "His ever-present humor calmed me. He provided me and many others the support and mentoring necessary to make us better lawyers." Mr. Lyons and Mr. Blagg are two of a long list of lawyers and judges who tell stories of how Hippo helped them to get started in the legal profession and kept them going straight afterwards.

Another way to understand his work for young people is to remember the softball team called the 144th Hippos. For over twenty years he sponsored the team and its players grew up to become accountants, lawyers, U.S. Attorneys, judges, and members of Congress. Some of them are household names in San Antonio, TX. You may have heard of some of the players: Judge John Primomo, Tom Moore, Judge Raymond Angelini, Wayne Hampton, Ed Piker, Tyler Mercer, Larry Blackstone, Frank Kuhn, Pat Huffstickler, Glen Grossenbacher, Judge David Rodriguez, Raul Rios, Mike Fisher, Danny Lopez, Don Mach, Gilbert Carrasco, Mike Clark, Congressman Charlie Gonzalez, Judge Ed Prado, Van Hilley, Mel Spillman, Judge Sol Casseb III, Joe Casseb, Carroll Barber, and Judge David Berchelman.

When they won first place in their Fall–Winter season 1982 they started calling Hippo, Owner Hippo Steinbrenner after George Steinbrenner of the New York Yankees. Since the team got a trophy, they decided to give Hippo a plaque with the inscription *Owner of the Year.*

Joseph Casseb worked as the State Court Coordinator for H. F. Garcia. He referred to the network of 20–30 young people following Judge Garcia as "his posse." The Judge's humor, humility, faith, and roots drew people to him, gave people hope. He was always looking and thinking of how to make things better. He had an eye on the future and future leaders.

During his life, Judge Hippo Garcia worked at four different levels of courts. To understand the four different courts the Judge worked in we can think about how a coach moves up to a higher level.

A coach begins training middle school kids and his teams compete with other middle school teams in the immediate area. That's like the District Attorney's (DA's) office working locally. This was Hippo's first job as a lawyer.

If they want to, middle school coaches can advance to more challenging high school teams. A high school coach instructs teenagers. He competes in a larger territory and enjoys tougher competition against neighboring high school teams in nearby cities. If an attorney wants to, he can file as a candidate to be elected county judge. The Bexar County Court-at-Law #2 was Hippo's second court.

A college coach trains young adult students from everywhere. He introduces them to the adult world while demonstrating honest ways to win their games. A professional coach trains hired players for national competition. As a coach advances from one level of the game to the next he operates in a larger territory, challenges stronger competitors, and faces more complicated game plans.

Hippo Garcia advanced to district and federal court. (See an outline of his four courts' functions p. 36.) When he was appointed to the 144th Judicial District Court in 1974, Hippo presided over trials for felony cases carrying sentences for one year to life in jail or death. Holding peoples' lives in his hands. Hippo said it was a calling second only to the ministry or medicine. He held this office until 1979.

This is an example of the kind of cases he heard in the District Court. Eight days after his swearing-in ceremony for the 144th Court, Judge Garcia presided over a kidnapping trial. Two-year-old Lisa Guerra disappeared from her home June 27, 1973. Massive searches by police and citizen volunteers failed to develop any clues in finding the child, last seen in her front yard with neighbor children. Almost a year later an anonymous tip led them to the home of Helen and Jesse Gomez where they discovered Lisa with a short, dyed haircut. Helen Gomez pleaded guilty and made her excuses for the kidnapping. She even attempted to adopt the child. Garcia sentenced her to ten years in prison.

Two days later Judge Garcia presided over a double murder of a 29-year-old mother, Gloria Costello and her 12-year-old daughter Teresa on June 7, 1974. The girl's brother Joe (age 2) and sister Gloria (age 5) were sleeping outside in the car and escaped through the darkness to a relative's home. The little children provided the first name of the murderer to the police. That information became essential to the investigation. David E. Palomo received a life sentence in prison for the murder of the mother and an additional 20 years for the daughter's killing from Judge Garcia.

Even later, the leader of a ring of professional thieves, was tried, convicted and sentenced in Judge Garcia's 144th District Court. Mary Lerma had acted as a police informant for thirty years, and had thus been able to elude the law. Lerma and her husband recruited and trained other thieves in special sessions. Their shoplifters operated in all major Texas cities and Mexico. One day they looted $16,000 in merchandise, easily stealing $200,000 a year according to the assistant district attorney at the time.

Hippo had fun times too. Friends planned a huge 50th birthday party for him at the courthouse, the first one ever celebrated there. Mrs. Celeste Casseb, spouse of Attorney Sol Casseb III, a sponsor of the event, filled the jury box with mariachis and the two attorneys' tables with treats. More than 100 wall-to-wall well-wishers came to the *Casa Colorada* (nickname for red brick courthouse) for the party.

*Hippo's Friends Circa 1970*
*Top Row L to R*
*Hippo Garcia, Phillip Chavarria, Tony Ferro, Anthony Nicholas,*
*Stanford Smith, Fred Semaan, Roy Barrera, Perry Smith.*
*Seated L to R*
*Mrs. Ferro, Virginia Nicholas, Norma Fink, Mrs. Semaan,*
*Carmen Zendejas Barrera, Nancy Smith.*

Margaret Montemayor, longtime Bexar County District Clerk and chicken-chef-supreme, tells stories of the Judge's bimonthly picnics in her office. The night before she fried four chickens and built a mountain of potato salad for their breakaway events. Judges and staffers chipped in and made themselves at home. Garcia served as master of ceremonies at these good times.

Margaret knew the Judge's favorite hangouts after work: the Barn Door and the Red Carpet restaurant. She's quoted him, "At 230 pounds, I'm living up to my name." Margaret Montemayor remembers how their fun times, jokes, and little pranks acted like oil in their machine. The team working for Judge Garcia repaired people in trouble. They heard as many disasters as emergency room workers. Humor and their family spirit kept them sober, safe and sane. It made them more creative, more productive in their work.

One day Margaret decided to ask Judge Garcia why he never married. He replied, "In my case, it wasn't necessary."

Bexar County District Attorney Susan Reed commented that Judge Hippo Garcia was not merely unusual; he was one of a kind. She said, approximately 20+ students and young professionals surrounded him much of the time. He gave his free time, abilities and money to help these people launch their careers. She indicated that there was no one like this before him and no one like this has come after him. Judges and attorneys are helping one, two or three young people not a whole troupe, not nonstop. Asked about all those after work, overtime sessions Reed said seriously, "Hippo did not see that as work. He saw that as life. Many of the friends we have today are because of the friendships he shared and built up among us. He was a dear friend, irreplaceable."

Most systems need improving. Aware of this need, the regular Bexar County Grand Jury prepared a written report requesting several reforms in the legal system. Judge Garcia was pleased to receive this unusual report. He stated that part of it had been under discussion by several judges earlier. He assured the public "something will be done." The Grand Jury requested: consistency in the size of bonds for the same type of offenses, uniformity in sentences for the same type of crimes, information on how to make bonds in Spanish and English, an educational program on the penal code for students and parents alike. Hippo made every one of these changes happen.

The Outstanding Alumnus Award was presented to Judge H. F. Garcia by St. Mary's University School of Law at the annual Law Day celebration March 29, 1980, in recognition for his contributions to the justice system. What a party with music, good food, and champagne all around!

Throughout his five years in the 144th Judicial District Court, nothing, nobody prepared H. F. Garcia for the approaching menace waiting on his long journey ahead.

# One Life—Four Courts—Fifty Years

## District Attorney's Office 1952–1964 A Hired Position

- » Prosecutes people accused of crimes against the safety of local individuals, families, and property
- » Assists victims of crime in getting compensation: DWIs, hot checks, kidnapping
- » Cooperates with local law enforcement and social service agencies: child abuse, family violence

## County Court At Law #2 1964–1974 An Elected Position

- » Tries civil cases where the money involved is low
- » Decides the official determination of wills
- » Tries misdemeanor criminal cases: shoplifting, reckless driving without injuries, public intoxication
- » Hears appeals from the Justice of the Peace and City Courts

## 144Th Judicial District Court 1974–1979 An Appointed Position

- » Hears all federal cases both civil and criminal: murder, armed robbery, obscenity with a child
- » Monitors the testimony of witnesses
- » Rules on admissibility of evidence
- » Settles disputes between defense and prosecuting attorneys
- » Creates new rules if standard procedures do not exist

## Federal Court Western District Of Texas 1980–2002 An Appointed Position

- » Tries cases in violation of the Constitution of the United States and federal laws
- » Hears cases between citizens of different states for amounts of more than $75,000
- » Rules on cases of bankruptcy, patent disputes, violations of maritime laws
- » Enforces federal laws to protect federal rights
- » Hears cases between U.S. citizens and citizens of different countries

# New People

Van G. Hilley was voted one of the Top 10 lawyers in San Antonio by his peers in *the Scene in San Antonio* 2005 magazine poll and has been a Texas Super Lawyer since 2003.Mr. Hilley's firm specializes in criminal defense. He also handles family law and probate matters.

Judge John F. Onion has spent 22 years on Texas' highest criminal court, the Texas Court of Appeals. He is a specialist in cases involving public officials who have broken the law and other sensitive matters.

Judge James R. Nowlin was sworn in as United States District Judge of the Western District of Texas on November 6, 1981. He had served as a member of the Texas House of Representatives 1967–1971 and 1973–1981.

Judge John Primomo is a U.S. Magistrate Judge. He worked as a briefing attorney for Judge H. F. Garcia Oct 1980—June 1988. Is a co-director of Camp Discovery, a summer camp for children with cancer. He mentors a student at Harlandale High School in San Antonio.

The Honorable Susan D. Reed is the first woman to be elected Criminal District Attorney of Bexar County, Texas. She served as judge of the 144th District Court of 12 years. Susan D. Reed has created several new resources for the safety of Bexar County residents: the Elder Fraud Unit, Bexar County Family Justice Center (the first and only such center in the State), Bexar County National Campaign to stop Violence (a unique educational program for seventh and 8th grade students).

# New Places

The Grand Jury is a group of people selected to decide whether someone should be charged (indicted) for a serious crime. It is called the Grand Jury because it has more jurors than the twelve found on a trial jury. It is used in the federal system only in the United States.

*Judge Roy R. Barrera Jr. Follows Judge Hippo Garcia to the 144th Judicial District Court*
*From L to R*
*Governor Bill Clemens, Roy R Barrera Jr (Judge), Judge Hippo Garcia.*

# Chapter 4: Works Consulted

Alvarado, Jennifer. San Antonio Parks and Recreation. Telephone interview. 18 Jul 2011.

Barrera, Roy R., Sr. Personal interview. 8 July 2011.

Barrera, Roy R., Sr. Personal interview. 19 July 2011.

Barrera, Roy R., Sr. Personal interview. 18 June 2012.

Beere, Jean. "Letting Go of Your Sacred Space." *Reflections Along the Way.* Spring/Summer 2011: 18–19.

Bexar County official website. <www.BexarCounty.org>

Black, Michael J. "Judge Hippo Garcia and the Fair Administration of Justice." *San Antonio Lawyer.* September–October 2000: 4–5.

Brenner, Susan, and Lori Shaw."What is a grand jury?" <http://campus.udayton.edu/~grandjur/faq/faq1.htm>

Casseb, Joseph. Personal interview. 1 July 2011.

Clift, Cecil. "Embezzler ordered to repay $119,316." *San Antonio Express-News* 19 September 1983, p. 6A.

Davenport, Joe. "DA Aide Garcia switching to other side of table." *San Antonio Express-News* 18 December 1963, p. 10A.

Diehl, Kemper. "Garcia almost sure Grace successor." *San Antonio Express-News* 10 September 1964, p. 1A.

"District Attorney, equivalent and related titles and offices." Wikipedia, 6 June 2011.

"Federal Courts and What They Do." <http://www.fjc.gov/public/pdf.nsf/lookup/FCtsWhat.pdf/$file/FCtsWhat.pdf>

Goldstein, Goldstein & Hilley. <http://www.goldsteingoldsteinandhilley.com/>

Gonzales, Jill. "What Does A District Court Judge Do?" *Wise Geek Clear Answers for Common Questions.* <www.wisegeek.com>

Grover, Nell Fenner. "Jury urges bond reform." *San Antonio Express-News* 23 October 1975, p. H 3A.

Hilley, Van. Personal interview. 2 February 2011.

Kristi, Renee. "Types of Felony Crimes in Texas." <http://www.ehow.com/list_6815118_types-felony-crimes-texas.html>

McCrory, James. "Coalition endorses Albidress." *San Antonio Express-News* 9 September 1964, pp. 1A, 12A.

McCrory, James. "Demos nominate HF Garcia." *San Antonio Express-News* 10 September 1964, pp.1A, 16A.

Montemayor, Margaret. Personal interview. 12 September 2011.

Nelson, Tom. (1982, January 7) Hippos pin new name on judge. *San Antonio Express News* p. 5B.

Nowlin, Judge James R. <http://www.cemetery.state.tx.us/pub/user_form.asp?pers_id=3278>

Primomo, Judge John W. <http://www.txwd.uscourts.gov/general/judges/biographyview.asp?bID=25>

Ramsey, Ross. <www.chron.com/CDA/archives/archive.mpl/1994_1182037/profile-john-f-onion-judge-is-a-specialist-in-sens.htmlRamsey>

Randell, Hamilton. Administrative Supervisor Bexar County Court at Law. Telephone Interview. 2 September 2011.

Reed, Judge Susan D. Personal interview. 29 September 2011.

Reed, Judge Susan D. Bexar County District Attorney's Office. <http://www.bexar.org/da2/>

Rodriguez, Judge David J. Personal interview. 14 July 2011.

Staff writer. "H. F. Garcia takes office." *San Antonio Express-News* 15 September 1964, p. 16C.

Staff writer. "10 years for kidnapping." *San Antonio Light* 9 January 1975, p. 1A.

Staff writer. "Lisa Guerra's kidnapper gets 10 years in prison." *San Antonio Express-News* 9 January 1975, p. 2D.

Staff writer. "S.A. man given life term." *San Antonio Light* 17 January 1975, p. 8A.

Staff writer. "Shoplift leader nabbed." *San Antonio Express-News* 13 May 1977, pp. 1 & 10A.

Terry, Eric. "Just a Closer Walk with Thee Honorable Hippo." *San Antonio Lawyer* September-October 2000: 6–13.

Texas Government Code. Chapter 24 District Courts, subchapter A article 24.245. 2005. <*www.statutes.legis.state.tx.us/docs/GV/htm/GV.552.htm*>

*Texas Uniform Jury Handbook,* as authorized by Chapter 23 of the Texas Government Code, September 2007.

Staff writer. "Shoplifting queen ready for prison." *San Antonio Express-News* 17 May 1977, p.1C.

West, Maurice. Personal interview. 12 July 2011.

Whitaker Center for Science and the Arts."What are the nine types of cases tried in federal court?" <http://wiki.answers.com/Q/What_are_the_nine_types_of_cases_tried_in_federal_court>

# Chapter 5

## Two Streets Away

A CHEERFUL MORNING MAY 29, 1979, turned into stark shock as people tuned into their TVs and radios for the morning news. Somber newscasters announced that Judge John H. Woods, presiding over the District Court Western Division of Texas, died from a single sniper's bullet outside his own front door. Judge Wood was the first U.S. federal judge slain in the twentieth century.

When the runaway Gregoria Rodriguez bought a house at 216 Lavaca Street did she say, "My grandson will become a legend in San Antonio?" No. Did her son, Hipolito #2, the rich young ranch boss turned hotel chef, imagine, "My son will be appointed a federal judge by the President of the United States?" Impossible. When young Hipolito #3 rocked on his front porch swing, did he dream he was looking directly at his future headquarters, the United States federal courthouse two streets away? Never, according to him.

Replacing Judge Woods took longer than replacing President John F. Kennedy after his assassination. When a President dies in office, the Vice President is sworn in automatically to take his place on the same day. For a murdered federal judge nothing like that exists. Only temporary substitutes fill in until a new judge is selected.

The search to find a new federal judge is a complicated process. The new judge must be acceptable to the people, to both political parties, and to the other judges.

The President of the United States selects a candidate from names political party leaders recommend and he sends the name to be confirmed by the U.S. Senate.

Famous people have allies they would like to see promoted. Groups like trial lawyers, labor leaders, law enforcement personnel, and legal scholars want to have a voice in the decision. Professional organizations from different sections of the country have their favorites.

Candidates must be interviewed by officials at the local, state and national levels. Senators want to question the candidates individually. The FBI screens each prospect.

So replacing a federal judge is a lengthy procedure. Gradually some candidates drop out of the race on their own. Others are eliminated after interviews and screenings.

For Hippo the confirmation process felt like a roller coaster. One day it seemed like his nomination was going forward. The next day it swerved in another direction. Any minute it could crash. Late in the process, Hippo described his feelings, "One day I was riding high, and the next day I was down in the depths. I'm just glad it's nearly over."

Hippo telephoned President Jimmy Carter's personal secretary, Susan Clough, to ask for advice on how to improve his chances. She suggested that he contact Republican friends and request their recommendation. He called Senator John Tower, a leading Texas Republican, who offered to help.

Normally the confirmation would have been completed before September 25, 1980, but the Senate Judiciary Committee chair, U.S. Senator Edward Kennedy, was waging an all-out campaign for the Presidency. This created a log jam of back work. Some individuals involved believe Kennedy stalled because he wanted to make his own judicial appointments after he won the election. This delayed the process even longer. Thirty federal judge candidates stood waiting for an answer. The long selection and confirmation process persuaded Hippo Garcia that his new assignment demanded a Rottweiler's courage and a lamb's patience.

Almost two years after Judge Wood's murder, President Jimmy Carter appointed Garcia and the U.S. Senate confirmed the appointment. An estimated 400–500 relatives and friends came to the dome of the Institute of Texan Cultures for his swearing-in ceremony October 17, 1981. The judge's mother, Francisca Garcia and his sister, Olga Rodriguez were among the special guests. Mrs. Garcia presented her son with a new robe. Hippo thanked President Jimmy Carter, Senator Lloyd Bentsen, Senator John Tower and all the wonderful people who had supported him. "The pay is good in this new job," said Hippo, " and the fringe benefits are better—benefits like walking on water."

He was now the first Hispanic Federal Judge of the U.S. District Court Western Division of Texas, a district that reached from San Antonio to El Paso, a total of 91,000 square miles.

Roy Barrera, Sr.'s daughter, Carmen Barrera Ramirez (Hippo's first godchild) worked as Hippo's Administrative Assistant for eight years. She recalls a joke her dad played on her the second day at the Federal Court. A man in dirty clothes and ragged socks showed up at her dad's office asking how to get into Hippo's office to congratulate him on his appointment. Roy recognized him as "Boots," a vagrant attorney suffering with alcoholism so advanced he stopped showering, shaving, and changing clothes. He told "Boots" his daughter worked for Judge Garcia. He told him "Introduce yourself, ask about her family, and she will get you in to see the Judge."

Boots walked to the Federal Courthouse, a few blocks from Barrera's office. He took the elevator upstairs and marched straight up to Carmen's desk. Shocked when she saw this man, she couldn't imagine how he got in. He began asking about her family, told her why he had come and that he needed to congratulate Hippo in person. Carmen's brain went limp. Just then, Hippo came into the doorway and called out, "Boots!" He gave him the man a great *abrazo*, took him into his inside office, served him coffee with cream and sugar. They talked for an hour and a half while Carmen studied the Judge's work piled high on her desk. From that second day until his last day, he never turned any person away who came to see him, to ask for his advice, or to tell him something.

One day Carmen asked the Judge directly, "How come you hired all new people for this office? None of us, not John Primomo, Marilyn Primomo, Mark Deitz nor I have any experience at Federal Court."

"Because I do not want someone coming in telling us what to do. I want all of us to learn this together." He was a lifelong learner.

Carmen Barrera Ramirez remembers a trial that affected her directly. Her husband Richard, a dentist, worked in Hebbronville, Texas two days a week. Every Monday night, after a long day's work, she picked up her baby girl, and went to the same restaurant, sat at the same table and had the same waitress. The waitress recognized that baby Margo was hungry and always brought her a small glass of water, a small glass of milk, a half cup of soup and crackers without waiting to be asked. She could imagine Carmen's workload, fatigue, and loneliness for her husband. The waitress's thoughtful attitude impressed Carmen, and she learned they each had two boys in the same school.

One morning Carmen saw the waitress sitting outside the courtroom and learned she had been arrested on drug charges. They recognized each other, but couldn't talk. Carmen went into the Judge's office, knelt next to his desk, told him the story, and begged for his help. He thought the waitress would be in prison twenty-two months. Carmen felt heartsick thinking about little kids motherless for twenty-two months, suffering from the crimes of adults.

During the trial, the facts showed the waitress had been caught in a sting operation, had accepted cocaine from an undercover agent who tempted her when she was exhausted. He hoped she would lead him to a neighborhood drug dealer. However, she knew nothing about dealers or selling drugs. Hippo gave her probation instead of prison. Her boys grew up well and strong, without serious problems.

Brackenridge High School teachers wanted promising students to do their internships in the Judge's office. The rules say that students must be in college or law school to work for a federal judge. No matter, Judge Garcia took them in anyway, invited them to attend his trials and practice writing outlines of the proceedings. He explained everything afterwards. In other words, he made a place for them even though he could not give them work from his office. Later he helped serious students to locate jobs. A group of political science teachers, lawyers, and Hippo wanted young people to understand the trial procedure. They created simulated trials sponsored by the Brackenridge High Political Science Club complete with handcuffs, defense and prosecuting attorneys, witnesses and a presiding judge. The *San Antonio Express News* covered their "trials."

A teacher at Burnet Elementary (one of the schools Hippo attended) told him, "Some parents never come to school for their child's show-and-tell. Will you send your staff here once a year to be make-believe parents for these children? We can't leave them alone all the time." The Judge agreed that leaving little kids alone hurt too much. The courthouse was only three streets away from the school. Some of his staff went to Burnet School to substitute for parents who couldn't come; others went to read with the children. Katy Jones, Burnet principal at the time, remembers the day they hosted "Here comes the Judge." After the program, the students served their guests lunch in the school cafeteria.

THE SAN ANTONIO LIGHT

Thursday, Nov. 20, 1980

San Antonio Light

*Judge Eats Lunch With Burnet Students*

During his twenty years in federal office, some of the meanest crooks the Judge faced were those who taught crime to younger relatives. Hippo was lenient with those he knew would improve their lives, but he was harsh with others who were vicious or recruited young people for crimes.

Pedro Vargas initiated his nephew Leroy Vargas Sosa (age 17) into bank robbery and murder. Pedro Vargas TDCJ #000778 has lived in prison since he was sentenced to death by H. F. Garcia. Vargas contends he is mentally retarded. No expert has ever proven he is mentally retarded. At the time of his trial he was illiterate, something that a person can change.

Investigators said without the nephew's brave speaking out against his uncle it would have been difficult to convict Vargas because both wore masks during the robbery. Leroy Vargas Sosa pleaded guilty and was tried as an adult.

Another case of family crimes involved five brothers, one of them a police officer. Five Lopez brothers and three friends joined up in marijuana and cocaine smuggling. They hired three former police officers to act as security guards for their drug operation. They pleaded guilty. Guilty of smuggling drugs, guilty of using an interstate facility to aid racketeering enterprises and guilty of wrecking their families and friendships. While there is no prison time for the last offense, this crime rains its own punishment down on every child and adult in its path.

The courts are like a defense system separating the dangerous persons from the innocent. This Judge managed the defense system by being severe with people in positions of trust who betrayed that trust.

Judge Edward C. Prado met Judge H. F. Garcia soon after Prado graduated from law school. Judge Prado wants people to realize that Hippo's story proves that we can be successful without ever being rich, without being tall and without ever being #1. He says Hippo's attitude moved about twenty-five couples to ask Hippo to be godfather to their sons and daughters. "Hippo was the truest, most real godfather that lived, beating Vito Corleone in every way possible," says Judge Prado.

Ninety-year old Oscar Flores said of Hippo, " I would lay my life in his hands. I never had a better friend. He was a gentleman, trustworthy, straightforward. He treated everyone alike. I am so proud to have known him." For twenty-five years Mr. Flores owned the Continental Restaurant known as City Hall Annex, one of Hippo's favorites.

Hippo Garcia overcame the spiky hurdles of language, war, prejudice and politics to become "The People's Judge." Before he realized it, however, his race was ending.

# New People

Charles Voyd Harrelson, a contract killer, murdered Judge H. Wood. He had murdered other people before he killed the Judge. He died of a heart attack in prison March 15, 2007. His son is the actor Woody Harrelson.

Senator John Tower was a Republican Senator from Texas 1961–1985. He served in the Navy during the Second World War, earned undergraduate and graduate degrees and served on many congressional committees. April 5, 1991, he died in a plane crash near Brunswick, Georgia.

Senator Lloyd Bentsen was a U.S. Senator and a Treasury Secretary. His immigrant family had little money when they moved to South Texas but they became successful in ranching and land development. He was elected County Judge at age 25, and from there climbed the political ladder quickly. He died at home on May 23, 2006.

Judge Edward C. Prado is a federal judge on the United States Court of Appeals for the fifth circuit. He has a long history of community involvement. A group of supporters tried to draft him to be nominated to the Supreme Court in 2005. He lives in San Antonio.

Vito Corleone is a fictitious family man pretending to be honorable and dedicated while ruling a criminal empire. *The Godfather* is the title of the book and the movie where he appears.

# New Places

The Institute of Texan Cultures is a museum belonging to the University of Texas at San Antonio. It honors all the immigrants who have come to Texas since the beginning.

# Chapter 5: Works Consulted

Beal, Bruce. "Two judges in S.A. to fed posts?" *San Antonio Light* 19 December 1979, p. 1.

Benjamin, Almedia, and Pauline Bonenberger. "All Brack Jury 'Convicts' Zuniga." *The Brackenridge Times* 27 November 1968, p. 3.

"John Howland Wood, Jr." *Biographical Directory of Federal Judges: Federal Judicial Center* <www.fjc. gov/history/judges.htm>

Bomar, Pat. "Demos nominate HF Garcia for judgeship." *San Antonio Light* 10 September 1964, p. 6.

Flores, Oscar. Telephone interview. 20 June 2012.

Gibbs, William J., Jr. "Nov. 4 marks 25 years since Childress' murder: Wilson County News. Section A: General News. 29 October 2008 <http://www.wilsoncountynews.com/article. php?id=21101&n=section-a-general-news-nov-4-marks-25-years-since-childress-murder>

"Scheduled execution—September 25th." *Gulf Coast Police News.* September 2006, p. 22.

Harrelson, Charles V. "Biography." <http://www.spartacus.schoolnet.co.uk/JFKharrelson.htm>

Holley, Joe. Lloyd Bentsen. Texas Senator, Vice President. *The Washington Post* 24 May 2006 <http://www.washingtonpost.com/wp-dyn/content/article/2006/05/23/AR2006052300593.html>

"Jimmy Carter Library & Museum." <http://www.jimmycarterlibrary.gov/library/pres_materials.phtml#top>

Jones, Katie. Telephone interview. 18 June 2012.

Langley, Roger. "Senate panel delays Garcia's confirmation." *San Antonio Express-News* 5 June 1980, p. 2A.

Prado, Edward C. <http://en.wikipedia.org/wiki/Edward_C._Prado>

Prado, Judge Edward C. Personal interview. 10 Oct. 2011.

Primomo, Judge John. Telephone interview. 7 July 2011.

Ramirez, Carmen Barrera. Personal interview. 30 June 2011.

Ramirez, Carmen Barrera. Personal interview. 18 July 2011.

Sosa v. Dretke. United States District Court, W.D. Texas.

Slayman, E. J. "Hippo takes office as a US district judge." *San Antonio Express-News* 18 October 1980, p. 2A.

Staff writer. "No joy, no justification, no judges." *San Antonio Express-News* 2 December 1979, p. 5H.

Staff writer. "Ex–policeman to plead guilty of drug charge." *San Antonio Express-News* 13 April 1984, p. 18A.

Staff writer. "3 brothers of S.A. officer guilty of drug smuggling." *San Antonio Express-News* 1 May 1984, p. 13A.

Texas Execution Information Center News. 7 September 2011 <www.txexecutions.org> <http://webcache.googleusercontent.com/search?q=cache:3ZeLw4TMZUcJ:www.txexecutions.org/+Texas+Execution+Information+Center&cd=1&hl=en&ct=clnk&gl=us>

# Chapter 6

# The Longest Short Day

SOMETIMES PEOPLE WON'T ADMIT TO themselves or others that they're dying. Hippo worked every day until the day before he died. He never told his family he had a life-threatening illness.

A few friends did know about it and they tried to help him. They built a hand railing from his office into the courtroom. He started going home earlier, staying in bed longer. Even Olga, his sister and friend, did not know how sick he was until Van Hilley told her son David, "It's time for the family to take over." When Olga asked Hippo, "Why didn't you tell me?" he answered, "I thought I could get my strength back."

December 4, 2001, marked his 76th birthday. He felt decrepit. He went to a doctor and learned that he was at risk for a heart attack.

"Jimmy Carter appointed me for life, and I took him at his word," he said when his family and friends tried to get him to retire or slow down. He applied for senior judge status hoping to satisfy his family and friends.

His request was granted, and he received senior judge status beginning January 15, 2002. The same day he was admitted to the hospital and was told nothing could be done to help him. The hospital transferred him to Brighton Gardens nursing center where he died the same night. That evening Judge John Primomo, his wife Marilyn, Mark Murray, and two friends went to the nursing center to stay with him. They talked and tried to joke with him, but he was uncomfortable. Even so, he was as much his normal self as he could be under the circumstances.

Judge Primomo cannot remember anything Hippo said that night. Although they were like father and son, they had not talked about dying and death. The Primomos left about 9:00 P.M. Soon after returning home, John felt the need to return to Brighton Gardens. He did not want his friend to be alone that night. Frank Kuhn came by later. After Frank left, Hippo fell asleep.

John remembers, "I laid down in the lounge chair next to his bed. I began to doze off; Hippo's sleep was fitful at times, not like he was in pain but dreaming. I held his left hand through the railing of his bed. Shortly before he died, Hippo suddenly made the sign of the cross, as if he saw something or knew the end had come. Shortly thereafter, Hippo vomited and stopped moving. I ran toward the nurses' station to summon help. I waited outside his room while the nurses were with Hippo. Within minutes they came outside to tell me he was dead." It was 3:55 A.M.

Dr. Herberto J. Garza telephoned Olga to say her brother died. Judge Primomo waited for Olga and her son David to arrive. They all saw him again after the nurses changed the bedding.

Judge John W. Primomo, who stayed with him all that last night wrote, "People often confuse being religious with being spiritual. Hippo was both religious and spiritual. He was a devout Catholic, but his Christianity was not measured by the number of times he attended Mass or received Communion. Hippo saw all as equal, gave to those in need, and loved unconditionally. Of those who were his closest friends, all of us miss him, smile at the many, many Hippo stories, and treasure the honored memory of a man unlike anything this life will ever see again."

Three funerals followed in the next three days. The first informal wake was held at night in San Fernando Cathedral. People packed the place: family and friends, friends of family and friends, neighbors, street people, and roughly carved men in jeans, denim work jackets, and cowboy boots. Some men leaned over the pews in front of them, crying. Newcomers were amazed at the sight.

Father David Garcia, known for his lively disposition took the microphone saying, "If it takes all night, we are here to tell all the stories. Come up to the mike." Beginning with Lila Marshall, Hippo's 92-year-old fourth grade teacher, they told their tales. School stories. War stories. Courtroom stories. Street stories. Jailhouse stories. They decorated each of the glorious mysteries of the rosary with more stories. The evening rose into a celebration memorial. His people thought about his life as they listened to each other and prayed the rosary out loud together. They honored his dying and death as a natural rhythm of life.

The next morning a formal funeral was held at San Fernando Cathedral. Black suits, starched white shirts, black and silver silk or bolo ties outfitted the men. Women dressed in navy blue or black or black and white dresses. Some wore suits. Others wore black arm bands. The Mayor, City Council members, attorneys, courthouse staff, St. Mary's University Law School professors and students, police officers, firefighters, press, radio and TV reporters came to pay their respects, to celebrate his life. Clergy and acolytes wore white and gold silk Easter vestments. The coffin holding the body was wheeled in and a solemn sung mass began. In this church, his Christian life began, and here its completion was celebrated with silver trumpets, violins, songs, flower wreaths, bright lights, and candles. Mass ended with *In Paradisum*. Soaring and peaceful, the choir repeated the refrain several times, as the body was wheeled out of the church, and carried down the stone steps to the waiting hearse. "May angels lead you into paradise; upon your arrival, may the martyrs receive you and lead you to the holy city of Jerusalem. May the ranks of angels receive you, and with Lazarus, the poor man, may you have eternal rest."

The third, a state funeral happened in Austin the next day. A state funeral is more formal than a wake, more somber than a church funeral. Because military and political powers play important roles, a state funeral emphasizes protocol and solemnity. War and politics are forces that give us different kinds of meaning. States honor their heroes for different reasons than individuals or communities of faith do. The State's interests are in loyalty, dedication to the state or nation, and the highest level of job performance. Flags, bugles, color guards, and 21-gun-salutes honor a citizen of the highest caliber. Judge Garcia wanted to be buried near Barbara Jordan, whom he admired. She was the first black state senator since 1883. He got his wish. Their resting places are one row, one grave apart at the Texas State Cemetery.

Recalling it, Hippo's friend Van Hilley said, "Look at his gravestone. That says it all."

Hipolito F. "Hippo"
Garcia
DEC 4 1925—JAN 16 2002

1943–1946
United States Army, 3rd Armored Division

1951
Admitted to State Bar of Texas

1952–1964
Bexar County District Attorney's Office

1964–1974
Judge, Bexar County Court-at-Law No. 2

1974–1979
Judge, Bexar County 144 Judicial District Court

1980–2002
United States District Judge Western District of Texas

*First Mexican-American appointed*
*to the federal bench in the*
*Western District of Texas*
*"To give dignity to a person*
*is above all things."*

# *Epilogue*

Soon after his three funerals, some judges wanted to rename San Antonio's Durango Boulevard after Judge Garcia. A friendly controversy followed because Durango is a historic street with a musical name. Public meetings, private meetings, newspaper articles, television and radio broadcasts wrestled with the dilemma. In the end, Durango Boulevard was subtitled Judge H. F. Garcia Boulevard The letters were so small a driver had to be up close to read them.

Four years later, people decided something more visible was needed, and they named the first federal building and United States Courthouse in Bexar County on 615 E. Houston Street after Judge H. F. Garcia. More celebration, more remembrances followed. No one walks by without seeing his name on a large marble monument naming the first San Antonio courthouse for him. Inside hangs a life-sized portrait of Judge H. F. Garcia. You cannot miss the morning sunshine in his eyes. The day the portrait was hung Judge James Nowlin said, "It is now our charge to keep his memory alive in our hearts and through our lives to reflect his decency and values, to dedicate ourselves to the dignity of all persons regardless of who they are or where they may have come from." This book was written to help keep that memory alive.

After three years work, this historic courthouse was fully restored and renovated with green environmental features. July 6, 2012 Hippo's family, friends and admirers came again to the federal courthouse to rededicate it to Judge H. F. Garcia. U.S. Representative Charles A. Gonzales said, "I love the fact that this building will be here another 100 years and people will still be talking about Hippo Garcia."

## New Ideas

Senior judge status is a form of semiretirement for U.S. federal court judges. On attaining the age of 65 and 15 years of judicial experience, in the federal courts, the federal court judges may apply for the senior status. A senior judge retains the judicial office and works only part time with full salary of a federal judge. A senior judge can reduce the workload to 75 percent. However, a senior judge can also opt to keep a heavy caseload to maintain an office with a secretary and two or more clerks.

*In Paradisum* is an antiphon (short musical setting) from the liturgy of the Roman Catholic Church.

## New People

Barbara Jordan might be the best speaker ever to serve in the Texas legislature. When she taught at the LBJ School of Public Affairs at University of Texas, Austin, so many students tried to register for her classes that administrators started a lottery. Students holding the first 200 numbers drawn won the seats in her classes. Hippo and Barbara are loved and admired by many people.

## New Places

The H. F. Garcia Federal Building and Courthouse is a seventy-five-year-old *Beaux Arts* style landmark and a symbol of the continued federal presence in downtown San Antonio. Located across from the Alamo, the building holds a prominent position on Alamo Plaza.

The purpose of the renovation project was to update the mechanical, electrical, and fire protection systems. The restoration project preserved key historic features on the exterior and interior of the building. For example, workers rewired, cleaned and polished the ornate chandeliers to their original glowing condition.

# Chapter 6: Works Consulted

AliSkahir. "In Paradisum." *Heavenly Meditations*. 2010 <http://agonist.org/numerian/20100328/in_paradisum_heavenly_meditations>

Certificate of Death: Hipolito Frank Garcia. Filed 25 Jan. 2002. State of Texas, San Antonio Metropolitan Health District, Reg. Dist. No.0200409, File No. 2421363. Certifier: Heberto Garza, Jr. M.D.

Garcia, Hipolito Frank. ID [7132] 05/16/2011 <http://www.cemetery.state.tx.us/pub/user_form.asp?>

Garland, Brendham P., and Felicia Olin. *Emo's Great Story.* Springfield, Illinois: Tiny Spider Books, 2011.

Gonzalez, Charles A. The Honorable, United States House of Representatives, Rededication Ceremony for the Hipolito F. Garcia Federal Building and United States Courthouse. 6 July 2012.

Jordan, Barbara Charline. ID [6624] 11/11/2011 <http://www.cemetery.state.tx.us/pub/user_form.asp?>

Martin, Gary. "Judge Garcia to Slow Down." *San Antonio Express-News* 9 Jan. 2002, pp. 1A, 4A.

Mazurkiewicz, Agata. *Faure Requiem "In Paradisum".* Concert in Berne, May 2007. <http://www.youtube.com/watch?v=zuQXGA_BwY4>

Nowlin, Judge James R. Dedication Ceremony for the Hipolito F. Garcia Federal Building and United States Courthouse. Presentation of the Official Portrait of H. F. "Hippo" Garcia, United States District Judge, Western District of Texas. 6 Dec. 2004.

Primomo, John W. Judge. E-mail from the judge. 4 Oct. 2011.

"Rededication Ceremony for the Hipolito F. Garcia Federal Building & United States Courthouse." 6 July 2012. Program.

Rodriguez, Olga Garcia. Personal interview. 5 Oct. 2011.

"Senior Judge Law & Legal Definition." *Legal Definitions Legal Terms Dictionary*. 2009 ed. Flowood, MS: US Legal Forms, Inc. <http://www./definitions.uslegal.com>

# Index

32886845R00047

Made in the USA
Lexington, KY
05 June 2014